PLAYING JAZZ PIANO

BY BOB MINTZER

For an aspiring jazz instrumentalist, playing piano is perhaps one of the most important skills for developing a jazz vocabulary. The piano is the doorway into the world of harmony, melody and rhythm. Regardless of what your primary instrument is, you simply must learn to play the piano. I would not be able to play a good deal of what I do today on the saxophone if I had not established a solid relationship with the piano.

By acquiring piano skills, one can:
- Learn tunes more efficiently
- Explore the more colorful aspects of improvising on tunes
- Develop a more comprehensive relationship with the rhythm section
- Improve your time
- Help take the guesswork out of improvisation
- Develop a harmonic sound and style of your own

I've spent countless hours exploring on the piano, starting from a very early age. The ability to incorporate melody, harmony and rhythm on one instrument was such a revealing and gratifying experience. To play a chord and move the notes around, trying different bass notes against a chord, establishing a groove as the result of the interaction between the two hands, and to play a chord and see what sort of melodic material worked with that particular harmony kept me occupied for long stretches of time. At first, it was the sound and feeling of playing things I'd stumble upon that had an impact. Later, as I began to identify some of the things I was playing by name, I was able to find further continuity in my improvising and composing. But the real benefit came from playing these sounds and musical shapes and feeling the way certain things resonated in my gut and mind's ear. The content of this book comes from concepts I've discovered through playing the piano, listening carefully to the pianists on my favorite recordings, and emulating the great pianists I've had the great fortune to work with.

Bob Mintzer

Alfred Publishing Co., Inc.
16320 Roscoe Blvd., Suite 100
P.O. Box 10003
Van Nuys, CA 91410-0003
alfred.com

All etudes composed and arranged by Bob Mintzer
©2008 MINTZER MUSIC CO. (ASCAP) All Rights Reserved
Exclusive Worldwide Distribution by ALFRED PUBLISHING CO., INC.

ISBN-10: 0-7390-5402-3
ISBN-13: 978-0-7390-5402-4

Photographs courtesy of Ira Wunder

Any duplication, adaptation or arrangement of the compositions contained in this book requires the written consent of the Publisher.
No part of this book may be photocopied or reproduced in any way without permission.
Unauthorized uses are an infringement of the U.S. Copyright Act and are punishable by law.

TABLE OF CONTENTS

BOB MINTZER BIOGRAPHY

In the jazz world, Bob Mintzer is a household name, usually associated with being a saxophonist, bass clarinetist, composer, arranger, leader of a Grammy-winning big band, member of the Yellowjackets and educator.

Bob has written over 200 big band arrangements spanning a 34-year career, many of which are performed all over the world by both student and pro bands. His own big band has been nominated for four Grammy awards and won a Grammy for Best Large Jazz Ensemble recording in 2001 with *Homage to Count Basie* on the DMP label. Bob has recorded 26 solo CDs with both big band and small jazz ensembles. He is an 18-year member of the Grammy award-winning Yellowjackets, and has recorded 12 CDs with the band. Bob tours four months out of the year with the 'Jackets.

Bob has published four jazz etude books (Belwin Jazz), a solo transcription book (Belwin Jazz), a saxophone method book, four saxophone quartets, 200 big band arrangements (Belwin Jazz, Kendor Music), and has composed several pieces for orchestra. His "Rhythm of the Americas" piece for sax quartet and orchestra (or concert band) was premiered in 2001 by the American Saxophone Quartet and the National Symphony Orchestra at the Kennedy Center in Washington, D.C. His "Concertino for Tenor Saxophone, Strings and Winds" was premiered in New York City by the St. Luke's Chamber Ensemble in 1992.

In addition, Bob has had a diverse career as a free-lance musician in NYC. He has recorded with people like Steve Winwood, James Taylor, Aretha Franklin and Queen. He has toured with Buddy Rich, Thad Jones, Mel Lewis, Jaco Pastorius, Tito Puente and Eddie Palmieri. He's performed with the New York Philharmonic and the American Ballet Theatre. Bob has been on the faculty of the Manhattan School of Music and recently joined the faculty of USC in Los Angeles. He also performs 20 workshops at universities all over the globe annually.

PERFORMANCE NOTES

To use this book effectively:
1. Learn the notes slowly at first, then in tempo.
2. Learn to play the etudes with good time and a steady groove.
3. Strive for a feel that fits with the style of each etude
   (swing-triplet inflection, Latin even eighth-note feel).

However, always keep in mind that listening to world-class pianists like Red Garland, Bill Evans, Herbie Hancock, Hank Jones, McCoy Tyner and Eddie Palmieri (to name only a few) is an integral piece of this process. I listened and still do!

The 22 etudes utilize three basic categories:
1. Comping chords with the right hand and playing a bass line with the left hand.
2. Comping chords with the left hand and playing a melody with the right hand.
3. Comping chords with both hands.

Some of the later etudes incorporate both the second and third category, because a soloing pianist will typically combine single-note melodic lines with two-handed chordal motion.

Another important focus of this book is to illustrate how pianists employ a melodic quality to the formation of chord progressions, known as voicings. That is, the top note of each chord in a given progression will generally create a strong sense of melodic motion.

At the end of the book you will find a Chord Voicing Glossary reference section with a variety of more advanced chord voicings that I have written throughout the book. ***Transpose these chords to all keys.*** Keep in mind, there are countless variations of these chord voicings. By no means is this a complete method for learning to play jazz piano. It is merely a tool to help you get up and running, particularly if you play another instrument.

Bob Mintzer

Etude 1: Begin with This

(Comping chords with the right hand and playing a bass line with the left hand)

If you ask me, it all starts with the blues. *Etude 1* is a typical blues progression with a walking bass line in the left hand and an ostinato comp in the right hand. The interaction between the two hands sets up a nice swing feel; therefore, this is a good etude to begin the process. The focus is on developing proper independence and interdependence of hands. The bass line places the roots of each chord on the strong beats 1 and 3 and passing tones on beats 2 and 4. Check out the melodic quality of the bass line. It is this melodic quality that gives a nice sense of forward motion and color to a bass line.

The first chord voicing is a typical dominant 9th voicing with the 9th on top, dominant 7th under that, and 3rd on the bottom. You can also add an A (6th) under the B♭, which I do on some of the subsequent dominant chords. Like most of the other voicings, this one does not have the root of the chord in the voicing. It's not needed. It is more important to include color notes such as the 9th, 11th and 13th. Notice that the voicing in measure 2 is a standard 13th voicing, with the 13th on top and the 3rd and 7th below. This voicing has a nice spacious and colorful sound due to the large interval between notes and the presence of the 7th and 13th. By the eighth measure, I begin to configure the chords with a close interval in the center of the harmony surrounded by larger intervals. The A7(♯5) has a C next to a C♯. I think it is the dissonance of this minor 2nd interval framed by two consonant intervals of a major 3rd and perfect 4th that gives this voicing its unique sound. In measue 9, I use the same configuration with the D9 chord. In measure 23, the first chord is C13, where you will find two close intervals—D and C, and B♭ and A, separated by a major 3rd. This also creates a colorful voicing due to the dissonance surrounding consonance.

On this etude, strive to gain consistency on the quarter-note pulse, with the bass line played up on top of the beat but still in a relaxed way. It is the combination of playing "on top" of the time, but with a relaxed feel, that creates the sense of swing. Play this with a metronome with the ultimate goal being that your internal clock becomes the metronome. Having the ability to comp is something you will use frequently as a teacher, a composer experimenting with new ideas, and as a means of learning new tunes. And as a result of being able to play a walking bass line with chordal accompaniment, you will gain some serious insight into the world of the rhythm section, which, as a horn player, is invaluable information.

Etude 1: Begin with This

Etude 2: Add More Color

(Comping chords with the right hand and playing a bass line with the left hand)

For *Etude 2,* play with the same rhythm in the right hand as in *Etude 1.* However, there are a few major differences here:

(1) The top note on these various voicings forms melodic shapes. This melodic approach to chordal motion gives a nice sense of forward motion and a more colorful quality to the chord progression.

(2) The other device I use in this version of the blues is the sus chord. The sus chord incorporates the 4th degree in a dominant 7th chord. These chords are configured as major 7th chords a whole step below the root. For example: Cmaj7/D.

The sus chord has an open, airy quality that serves as a nice contrast to the traditional dominant 7th or 9th chord voicing. In measures 9 and 14, the sus chord resolves to a dominant 9th chord. The sus 4 moves to the third in each case. Notice how in any given measure the first chord moves in a melodic fashion to the second voicing. Graceful voice leading is an integral part of providing forward motion to any chord progression.

(3) The addition of 9ths, 11ths and 13ths to the chord voicings adds a good deal more color to the music. This more colorful harmonic setting allows for more varied and, ultimately, more interesting melodic information in your improvisations.

Etude 2: Add More Color

Etude 3: The Blues Basic Comp

(Comping chords with the right hand and playing a bass line with the left hand)

In many ways, this piece has a classic jazz quality. The dominant 7th ♯9 chords in the first four measures move down a half step and then up again. This creates a nice melodic motion to the voicings. The same type of motion continues throughout the piece, with the same two-measure phrase repeated through the two choruses of blues changes.

The dominant 7th ♯9 voicing is a great color alternative to a straight dominant 7th or 9th voicing. The half–whole diminished scale can be played over this voicing, with various configurations. For improvisation, you may also use these two approaches: root, minor 3rd, 4th, 5th and dominant 7th; or root, minor 3rd, major 3rd, 5th and dominant 7th as a melodic approach over this voicing. Notice that the voicing in the second chorus, beginning at measure 13, is different. For one thing, the top notes of the chords are higher than in the previous chorus. This makes for a lift in energy, and provides contrast from one chorus to the next. Secondly, the voicings in the second chorus have more of a spread as opposed to the closer voicings in the first chorus. This change will give the second chorus more of an open sound.

The interaction of the left-hand bass line and the chords played in the right hand sets up a nice half-time swing groove. Once you've got the notes down, play this piece many times in a row. You have now entered the world of swing!

Etude 3: The Blues Basic Comp

Etude 4: The Blues Right-Hand Solo
(Comping chords with the left hand and playing a melody with the right hand)

As you know, for a single-note instrumentalist it is quite beneficial to have the option with the piano to play a chord in one hand, and then play melodies that correspond to that chord with the other hand. Not only is this ability to hear the relationship between harmony and melody such an asset, but also being able to visualize all that you are playing is a great help. I've found this to be a handy way to get further into the twelve tones in a way that will ultimately allow you to hear and think music away from an instrument.

The rhythm of the left-hand chords is similar to the first two etudes, so by now you should be familiar with the sound and feel of this approach. For this etude, imagine that there is a bass player and drummer playing in your head, laying down a steady and energetic quarter-note pulse. The left-hand chords should be played in this context, with a relaxed precision and a somewhat percussive quality, or accent on all the attacks. The right-hand melodies should be played with a swing feel. Swing feel can be simply described as an implied eighth-note triplet feel. When playing eighth-note lines, the first of two eighth notes should have the value of a quarter note in a triplet configuration, and the second eighth played as the third eighth in the triplet.

Notice that the interaction of the two hands and the way they compliment each other rhythmically sets up the groove. There are places where both hands play on the same beat, but the majority of the piece finds the two hands independent of each other, very much like what a drummer does with his or her four limbs. To make an analogy to a drumset, it is the interaction between ride cymbal (on quarter notes), hi-hat (on 2 and 4), and bass and snare drum (frequently playing syncopated patterns) that a pianist creates when comping with the left hand and soloing with the right.

In this etude, there are three places where both hands come together to play a chord which sets up a sense of variety offering a contrast from the pattern of chords with the left hand and eighth-note melody with the right hand. This also is a nice way to create a pause or breath in the flow of notes. The first of these chords occurs at the end of measure 10, the second at the end of measure 12, and the last one at the end of measure 22, the third measure from the end. As the etudes progress, we'll get further into integrating two-handed chords and soloing. Melodic material in the right hand is straight from the be-bop vocabulary, both in terms of melodic and rhythmical shape. Notice that I never play the root or tonic of a chord on the strong beats 1 or 3. It is much more interesting and colorful to play either the 3rd, 5th, 7th, 9th or 11th on beats 1 and 3. In measure 13, there is a little eighth-note figure played in thirds that I think adds a nice sense of arrangement and variety to the etude.

Etude 4: The Blues Right-Hand Solo

Etude 5: The Blues Comp Chords

(Comping chords with both hands)

This one involves the two hands playing chordal figures using a series of stacked 4th interval voicings. The sound of these voicings is very flexible and open sounding. The root and 5th of each chord is played at the beginning of each phrase, thus adding a bass element to the "comp" and generally rounding out the harmony. Notice how the top note of the various voicings creates a nice melodic shape. So in a sense, this might be something that could be played as a piano solo or as accompaniment to another soloist.

On beat 2 of the second measure, I've implemented a C7(#9) chord. This chord is the 5 (V) chord to the tonic key of F. This is a device that works well any time you are playing over the tonic chord for a while and want to add some extra harmonic movement. Measures 9 and 10 contain a small side trip away from the C7(#9) tonality. This could also be described as a C pedal with a series of chords that don't actually relate to C7(#9), at least the two chords at the beginning of measure 10. What is created is an arc of chords with the top notes outlining the C half-whole diminished scale which does relate to C7(#9).

Play this piece slowly at first, trying to absorb the lush sound of these voicings. Eventually get the tempo up to a comfortable swing feel with triplet inflection in the playing of the eighth notes. Also try for a nice connection or legato between the chords. In order to do this, you must play the notes long and with precision. Do not hit the keys too hard. Rather, go for a round, full sound.

Another side adventure might be to take the first phrase and play it in all the different keys. This is one sure-fire way to insure that you will have this shape under you fingers and in your musical vocabulary when it comes time to play some piano. Pianists to listen to who play in this style are Herbie Hancock (Miles Davis recordings from the early '60s), McCoy Tyner (John Coltrane Quartet, early to mid '60s), and Cedar Walton (Art Blakey, mid '60s). When you listen to these artists, really try to focus on the inner notes in the voicings the pianist is playing.

Etude 5: The Blues Comp Chords

Etude 6: Rhythm Changes Comp with Bass Line

(Comping chords with the right hand and playing a bass line with the left hand)

Rhythm changes ("I Got Rhythm") in a harmonic progression, along with the blues, is one of the war horses of jazz improvisation. I strongly suggest you strive to play rhythm changes in a variety of keys and tempos. Once you learn this piece, play these changes in all keys as an exercise. Do it, you'll be glad you did!

In this etude, chords are played with the right hand and a bass line with the left. Like *Etudes 1* and *2*, try for a steady and forward-moving quarter-note pulse in the bass line and a nice crisp attack in the right-hand chords. Once again, the top note of the chord voicings forms a melodic shape that sits nicely on the chord progression. The rhythm of the right-hand chords against the bass line establishes a sense of swing that is so very characteristic of the bebop tradition. These rhythms create a sound that is reminiscent of a big band horn section. In fact, the highly seasoned jazz pianist Hank Jones comes to mind because he has the ability to improvise an accompaniment that in some ways is just as interesting as what the soloist is playing.

There is a lot to be gained as a horn player in learning piano language as it applies to forming melodic lines. A nice exercise might be to try singing a solo line while playing the piece. See if the vocal line can interact with and compliment the piano accompaniment in a musical way. This is the language of the soloist versus accompanist that is so very important and makes for the conversational aspect of jazz music.

As a point of reference, listen to one of the Yellowjackets recordings like *Mint Jam, Time Squared* or *Altered State* and see how pianist Russell Ferrante and I leave space to accommodate each other's playing. We constantly are tossing ideas back and fourth. Along with this conversational element, Russ is contributing to the groove in a big way with other devices he uses. Listen and check it out.

This page is intentionally blank to facilitate page turns.

Etude 6: Rhythm Changes Comp with Bass Line

Etude 7: Rhythm Changes Comp Chords
(Comping chords with both hands)

This etude is what a jazz pianist might play to accompany a soloist, or perhaps play as a piano solo. Once again, the top voice of each chord creates a nice melodic shape. The rhythms form a varied and swingin' accompaniment, very much like what a big band horn section might play on this groove. The pianists I like to play with are able to lay down a chord progression in this fashion, which creates an energetic sense of swing and forward motion. In the process they contribute to the groove, as well as respond to the soloist playing a rhythmical figure in the spaces between the soloist's phrases. Pay close attention to the way the notes in the voicings are distributed. Check out how they sound and feel. A good solid voicing has a nice ring to it while also being colorful and interesting in texture. These voicings are abounding in the more colorful notes, as in 9ths, 11ths and 13ths.

When playing this etude, try to imagine the drummer and bassist laying down a strong quarter-note pulse. This quarter-note pulse is the underlying foundation for which the rhythms are based. It's really all about the quarter note! Notice that at this tempo, any eighth-note movement should have a triplet feel rather than an even eighth feel. Playing voicings like these can open up your ears to the more interesting side of melodic playing. Challenge yourself to explore what scales go with each respective voicing.

Etude 7: Rhythm Changes Comp Chords

Etude 8: Rhythm Changes Right-Hand Solo
(Comping chords with the left hand and playing a melody with the right hand)

This 32-bar AABA-form etude is an opportunity to see how the pianist accompanies a soloist with certain chord voicings. Only in this case, it is the pianist soloing with the right hand and the accompaniment is with the left hand. Notice that the roots of the chords are seldom played—leave that to the bass player. But the combination of the rhythm and the distribution of the notes in the left hand, combined with the melody in the right hand, provides a complete package. As always, play along with the rhythm section in your head.

In measure 2, on beat 3, the right hand plays the ♭9 and then the ♯9 against the F7(♯9♯5) chord. This is a colorful, lush sound that resolves nicely to the major 6/9 chord on the downbeat of measure 4. In measure 5, on beat 3, there is a ♯11th which resolves to the perfect 5th on beat 4. The sound of the ♯11 on a strong beat against the B♭(♭9) chord is colorful and interesting.

At the beginning of the bridge, the etude breaks into two-handed block chords, which serve as a contrast to the single-note lines in the right hand. Also in this bridge you will find an occasional stab at the root of the chord. In measure 24, the last measure of the bridge, the right-hand melody actually outlines a tritone substitution to F7, so I use notes which spell F♯mi7 to B7. This technique works well against any dominant 7th chord with a ♯5 and ♯9. In measures 31–34, I employ a series of quartal harmonies, which are stacked fourth intervals that move somewhat randomly. This kind of harmonic motion generally calls for a more chromatic line in the right-hand solo. In measures 33 and 34, the right-hand melody involves a I-IV-V pattern that repeats a minor third apart. This device can be a nice departure from the more diatonic changes. It can create a sense of tension which, if resolved properly, can be very dynamic and effective. Check out the last two chord voicings in the last two measures. These voicings have almost every note of the half-whole diminished scale in them. A real ear opener!

Etude 8: Rhythm Changes Right-Hand Solo

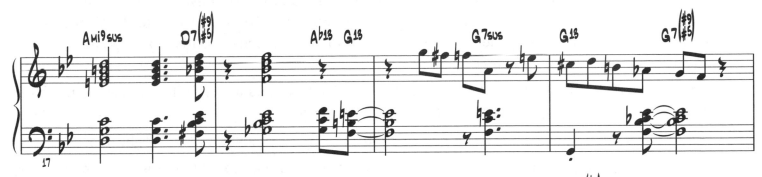

Etudes 9–17

The next nine etudes (9–17) are based on three different sets of standard chord changes and utilize the three different comping techniques: (1) comping chords with the right hand and playing a bass line with the left hand, (2) comping chords with the left hand and playing a melody with the right hand, and (3) comping chords with both hands.

The following comments apply to the next 9 etudes:

Once you've learned the notes, try for a nice feel and sense of swing. Playing these harmonic progressions typical of the American popular song of the '30s and '40s are crucial to developing a sound vocabulary in jazz music. When something in one of these etudes catches your ear, go a step beyond the page and try the following:

- Isolate the chord or series of chords and play the chord/progression in different keys to unlock the possibility of becoming more articulate with jazz harmony.

- Read the notes in the left hand and improvise off the chord changes with the right hand.

- Move the progression around in a variety of ways to achieve the flexibility to take a harmonic shape and utilize it in whatever key you may be playing in.

- Play a fixed rhythm in the right hand like a series of quarter notes, or quarter-quarter-quarter-quarter-quarter-eighth-eighth, which is a unifying element that will help organize your improvising skills.

Etude 9: Standard #1 Comp with Bass Line

(Comping chords with the right hand and playing a bass line with the left hand)

Etude 10: Standard #1 Comp Chords

(Comping chords with both hands)

Etude 11: Standard #1 Right-Hand Solo
(Comping chords with the left hand and playing a melody with the right hand)

Etude 12: Standard #2 Comp with Bass Line

(Comping chords with the right hand and playing a bass line with the left hand)

Etude 13: Standard #2 Comp Chords

(Comping chords with both hands)

Etude 14: Standard #2 Right-Hand Solo

(Comping chords with the left hand and playing a melody with the right hand)

Etude 15: Standard #3 Comp with Bass Line

(Comping chords with the right hand and playing a bass line with the left hand)

Etude 16: Standard #3 Comp Chords

(Comping chords with both hands)

Etude 17: Standard #3 Right-Hand Solo

(Comping chords with the left hand and playing a melody with the right hand)

Etude 9: Standard #1 Comp with Bass Line

Etude 10: Standard #1 Comp Chords

Etude 11: Standard #1 Right-Hand Solo

Etude 12: Standard #2 Comp with Bass Line

Etude 13: Standard #2 Comp Chords

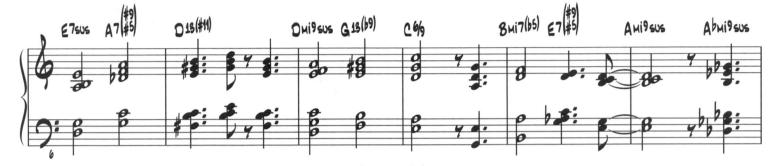

Etude 14: Standard #2 Right-Hand Solo

Etude 15: Standard #3 Comp with Bass Line

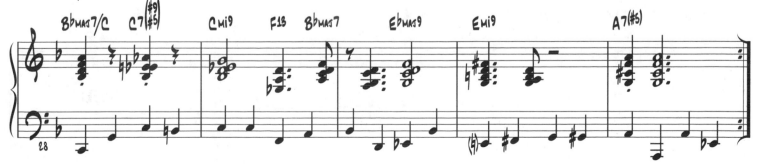

Etude 16: Standard #3 Comp Chords

Etude 17: Standard #3 Right-Hand Solo

Etude 18: Another Blues Right-Hand Solo

(Comping chords with the left hand and playing a melody with the right hand)

For *Etude 18,* as in the other etudes, there are places where both hands join together to play a two-handed voicing. You will find dominant 7 sus chords throughout this etude. In measure 16, there is a tritone substitution (instead of Fmi7/Bb7, I use Bmi7/E7).

Check out the sound and shape of the piece, and see how the two hands interact. There is a real conversational quality to the relationship between hands. One always compliments the other. When this same kind of empathy can happen between an instrumental soloist and the pianist, then you're really saying something. This is why it is so crucial that, as a horn player, you are familiar with the language of piano comping. With this familiarity comes the ability to truly converse with the pianist in a call-and-response fashion, constructing your phrases in a way that breathes and leaves room for input from the pianist.

I've found that accompanying instrumental students on the piano has increased my awareness of the relationship between piano and soloist. You can really feel if the soloist is phrasing in a sensible way from the piano chair. When a horn player constructs phrases that make good musical sense in their improvisations, it is easier to accompany on the piano. When the instrumentalist is over-playing, or playing in a way that is not in context, you have to work much harder at the piano to keep the music moving forward.

Etude 18: Another Blues Right-Hand Solo

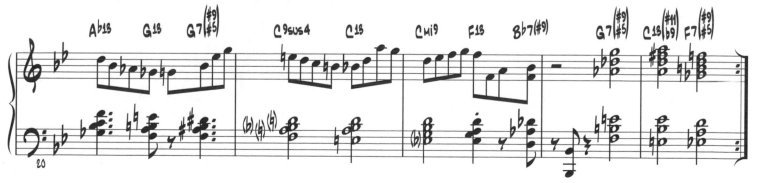

Etude 19: Another Blues Comp Chords
(Comping chords with both hands)

Etude 19 is a blues comp that might be played as an accompaniment to a horn solo. You could conceivably play this in a piano solo as well. The voicings are colorful and lush-sounding. Play this piece slowly and absorb the sound of the voicings and how they move. It is these types of chords that helped to open my ears as an improviser. They are abounding in 9ths, 11ths and 13ths. Many of the voicings also have a half-step interval somewhere in them, which creates a nice harmonic tension surrounded by more spacious intervals such as 3rds and 4ths. The stacked fourth interval sound demonstrated here is widely used by all the modern pianists, and is paramount to the jazz piano vocabulary.

Once you've learned the notes and can play the piece in tempo, play along to a metronome where the ♩=100. You can have the clicks on 1 and 3, or 2 and 4. Play off the quarter-note pulse by hearing the ride cymbal and walking bass line in your head.

If you can get this to feel good, you may be ready for your first piano jazz gig! Incidentally, think about notating these voicings for the horns—they will sound quite good. You might try writing a blues in this style for six horns (2 trumpets, 3 saxophones and 1 trombone). The main consideration here is that the notes lie in a good range for the instruments.

Etude 19: Another Blues Comp Chords

Etude 20: Ballad

(Combine: Comping chords with the right hand and playing a bass line
with the left hand, and comping chords with both hands)

This piece should be played at a slow tempo, ♩ = 60. The key to making this etude effective is to focus on playing in a legato fashion where there is a smooth connection between notes and a beautiful sense of phrasing. In general, all notes should be played long.

Try to think horizontally, moving gracefully from one chord to the next. You will find instances of inner motion, where a secondary melody is played and, if possible, bring these moving lines out a bit. In the 10th measure I use a G pedal with an ostinato chord progression that creates a sense of suspension for four measures. The ostinato rhythm continues in measures 14–17, but this time in the left hand.

What I tried to do with this piece is to provide a variety of textures from phrase to phrase. In a slow tempo like this, it is imperative that you play in a beautiful and interesting way. There is no place to hide when playing slow tempos. I sometimes think of making each phrase "sing."

Etude 20: Ballad

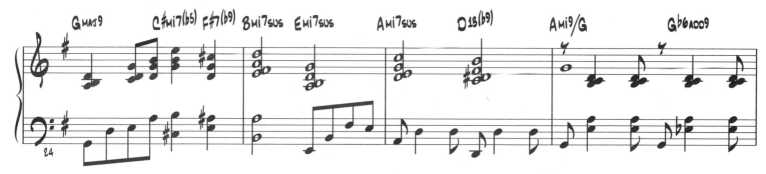

Etude 21: Latin Comp Chords

(Comping chords with both hands)

This etude is a blues comp that can be played in a cha-cha tempo. I wrote a tonic bass note on the "and" of beat 1 in alternating measures for rhythmical emphasis. Regarding feel or concept, try to play this one on top of the beat with an even eighth-note feel. Needless to say, it is essential to check out a few Latin piano recordings of artists like Eddie Palmieri and Tito Puente to see what this is all about. In the mean time, *Etude 21* is a piano etude to work on and absorb.

The first voicing is a Dsus7 and is sometimes called Cmaj7/D or simply C/D. One of the interesting things about this first voicing is the half-step interval at the bottom (C against B). I like the sound of this a lot. That little bit of dissonance provides a nice texture to an otherwise open-sounding voicing. I use this chord a lot in my writing.

In the 12th measure, the A7(#9#11#5) has an interesting sound. The inner voices are close together (C, D♭, E♭, F), thus creating a thickness and richness that has a lot in the way of rhythmical impact when played in this context. Play it and listen and you will hear what I'm describing. The syncopated quality of this piece can be somewhat challenging if you haven't had exposure to this kind of music. It should be played very deliberately with lots of weight given to each chord. Although these articulations are marked staccato, they should not be played too short but instead, with a fatness and funkiness—the staccato suggests separation, not duration.

Etude 21: Latin Comp Chords

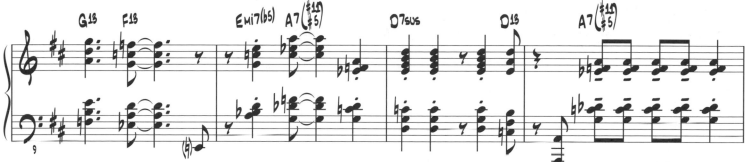

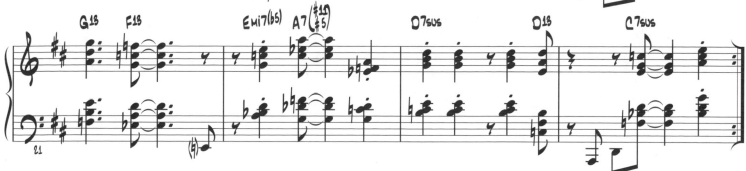

Etude 22: Latin Comp with Bass Line

(Comping chords with the right hand and playing a bass line with the left hand)

This etude utilizes a typical Latin bass line in the left hand combined with two commonly played comps, or montunos, in the right hand. It may take a minute to get this up and running rhythmically. But once you do, it feels really great to play. Practice it slowly and gradually increase the tempo. This is a good etude to play for as long as you can. The idea is to get to the point where you can play this on auto-pilot, not thinking at all about what you are doing. You can play with a metronome set at a variety of tempos, where the click is set to the half note.

The combination of left and right hand sets up one of the greatest and most interesting grooves that I know. Getting this groove into your bones will most certainly help your jazz playing, as well as help your sense of timing in whatever music you choose to play. With all the syncopated figures, a lot is implied rather than stated. The fact that the bass line hits on beat 4, rather than on the downbeat of the next measure, creates this beautiful floating sensation that propels the music along in such a cool way. Latin music is such an integral part of jazz music. Everyone should have some idea of how Latin rhythms function, particularly from the piano chair.

Hopefully these two Latin-based etudes will get you started. I strongly suggest you continue with the Latin groove and check out other Afro-Caribbean recordings!

Etude 22: Latin Comp with Bass Line

Chord Voicing Glossary

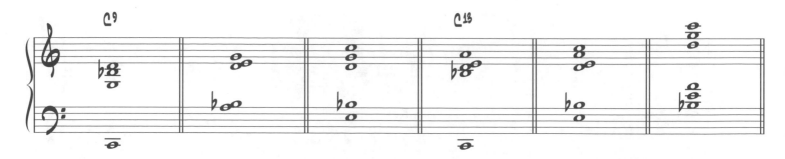

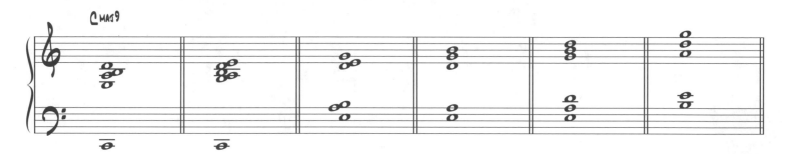

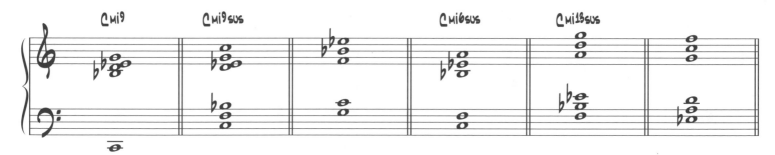

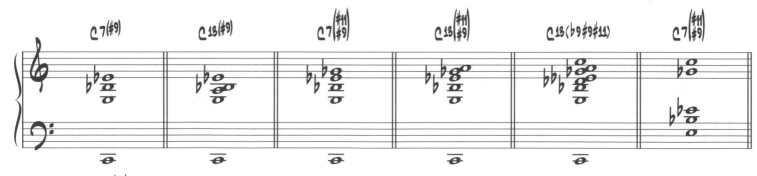

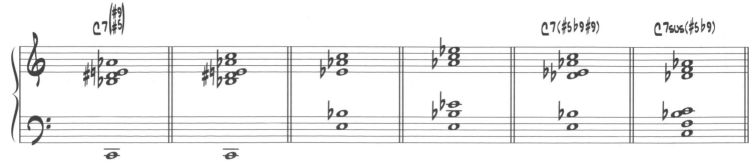

Bob Mintzer Selected Discography

As Leader

1980 *Horn Man* (Canyon Records)
1981 *The Source* (Canyon Records)
1984 *Papa Lips* (CBS Sony)
1985 *Incredible Journey* (DMP)
1985 *The First Decade* (compilation) (DMP)
1986 *Camouflage* (DMP)
1988 *Spectrum* (DMP)
1989 *Urban Contours* (DMP)
1990 *Hymn* (OWL)
1990 *The Art of the Big Band* (DMP)
1991 *I Remember Jaco* (Jive/Novus)
1991 *One Music* (DMP)
1991 *Departure* (DMP)
1993 *Only in New York* (DMP)
1994 *Twin Tenors* (Novus)
1995 *Big Band Trane* (DMP)
1996 *Live at Jazz Club Fasching* (Dragon)
1998 *Latin from Manhattan* (DMP)
1998 *Quality Time* (TVT)
2000 *Homage to Count Basie* (DMP) (GRAMMY™)
2003 *Gently* (DMP)
2004 *Live at MCG* (MCG Jazz)
2005 *In the Moment* (Art of Life Records)
2006 *Old School New Lessons* (MCG Jazz)
2008 *Swing Out* (MCG Jazz)

With the Yellowjackets

1990 *Greenhouse*
1991 *Live Wires*
1992 *Like a River*
1993 *Rynferyerlife*
1994 *Dreamland*
1995 *Blue Hats*
1997 *Club Nocturne*
2000 *Mint Jam*
2002 *Time Squared*
2004 *Altered State*
2005 *25*
2008 *Life Cycle*

As Sideman

1973 Buddy Rich *Ease on Down the Road*
1979 Sam Jones *Something New*
1977 Buddy Rich *No Jive*
1980 Buddy Rich *Live at Ronnie Scott's*
1980 Mel Lewis *Live at the Village Vanguard*
1981 Jaco Pastorious *Birthday Concert*
1982 Peter Erskine *Peter Erskine*
1985 Bobby McFerrin *Best of Bobby McFerrin*
1986 Steve Winwood *Back in the High Life*
1987 Marianne Faithfull *Strange Weather*
1988 Peter Erskine *Motion Poet*
1988 Lyle Mays *Street Dreams*
1990 Don Grolnick *Weaver of Dreams*
1990 Randy Brecker *Toe to Toe*
1991 Peter Erskine *Sweet Soul*
1991 George Gruntz *Blues 'n Dues Et Cetera*
1991 James Taylor *New Moon Shine*
1992 Special EFX *Global Village*
1992 GRP *Big Band*
1992 GRP *All Star Big Band* (Video)
1993 Michael Franks *Dragonfly Summer*
1993 GRP All Star Big Band *GRP All Star Big Band: Live!*
1994 GRP *All Star Big Band All Blues*
1995 Steve Winwood *Finer Things*
1995 Michael Franks *Abandoned Garden*
1998 Marilyn Scott *Avenues of Love*
1998 Nnenna Freelon *Maiden Voyage*

Learn **jazz concepts, improvisation** and **sight reading** for all instruments
from jazz legend **Bob Mintzer!**

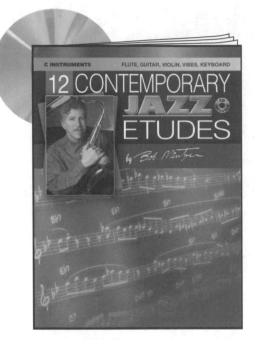

- **12 jazz etudes composed by Bob Mintzer in a variety of jazz styles, tempos, and time signatures**
- **Performance notes/tips for each etude to assist in interpretation and improvisation**
- **Play-along CD with a stellar rhythm section**
- **All books are compatible and written so they can be performed together!**

12 Contemporary Jazz Etudes
Book & CD

(ELM04011)	C Instruments—Flute, Guitar, Violin, Keyboards	$24.95
(ELM04012)	B♭ Tenor Saxophone and Soprano Saxophone	$24.95
(ELM04013)	E♭ Instruments—Alto and Baritone Saxophone	$24.95
(ELM04014)	B♭ Trumpet and Clarinet	$24.95
(ELM04015)	Bass Clef Instruments—Trombone, Baritone, Horn and Tuba	$24.95

also available from Bob Mintzer and Belwin Jazz:

The Music of Bob Mintzer:
Solo Transcriptions and
Performing Artist Master
Class CD
Book & CD

(0479B) $24.95

15 Easy Jazz, Blues
& Funk Etudes
Book & CD

(ELM00029CD)	C Instruments—Flute, Guitar Keyboards	$19.95
(ELM00030CD)	B♭ Instruments Tenor Saxophone and Soprano Saxophone	$19.95
(ELM00031CD)	E♭ Instruments—Alto and Baritone Saxophone	$19.95
(ELM00033CD)	B♭ Trumpet and Clarinet	$19.95
(ELM00032CD)	Bass Clef Instruments—Trombone, Baritone, Horn and Tuba	$19.95

14 Blues & Funk Etudes
Book & CD

(EL9604CD)	C Instruments—Flute, Guitar Keyboards	$26.95
(EL9605CD)	B♭ Instruments Tenor Saxophone and Soprano Saxophone	$26.95
(EL9607CD)	E♭ Instruments—Alto and Baritone Saxophone	$26.95
(EL9606CD)	B♭ Trumpet	$26.95
(EL9608CD)	Bass Clef Instruments—Trombone, Baritone, Horn and Tuba	$26.95

14 Jazz & Funk Etudes
Book & CD

(EL03949)	C Instruments—Flute, Guitar Keyboards	$24.95
(EL03950)	B♭ Instruments Tenor Saxophone and Soprano Saxophone	$24.95
(EL03952)	E♭ Instruments—Alto and Baritone Saxophone	$24.95
(EL03951)	B♭ Trumpet	$24.95
(EL03953)	Bass Clef Instruments—Trombone, Baritone, Horn and Tuba	$24.95

Belwin JAZZ
a division of **Alfred**

All prices in US Dollars and subject to change.

Alfred

alfred.com